THE PARIS INTERIOR
HERBERT YPMA

THE PARIS INTERIOR
HERBERT YPMA

conran
OCTOPUS

CONTENTS

INTRODUCTION

There are so many books about Paris: the cafés of Paris, the bridges of Paris; books on Paris fashion, Paris history, Paris monuments, Paris lifestyle and, inevitably, books on Paris apartments and interiors.

Yet most books that have been published about Parisian interiors start with the premise that there is in fact no such thing as 'the Paris interior' – that the approach to architecture, design and decoration found in the premier city of France is so widely varied in scope that there can be no 'common thread' to the style.

I disagree. Whether in an ad for perfume or a film by the likes of Polanski or Bertolucci, we recognize a Parisian setting before we are told – if indeed we are told at all. Why? Because there is a visual language at play that is unique to Paris. Like a language, too, it is ultimately a composition of its parts: its furniture, fabrics, objects and details are as distinctive as verbs, adverbs, nouns and adjectives.

The Paris interior is not just about tables, chairs, cabinets and candlesticks, however. It is a cultural phenomenon, a three-dimensional synthesis of an illustrious past rich in patronage of the arts. The beauty, charm and sophistication that we respond to are not just matters of taste but also matters of tradition – a tradition filtered through France's singular history.

Each idea, each direction, each fashion, has been tested, re-tested and refined by successive generations. Unlike the French Revolution, the change undergone by the Paris interior has been slow and gradual, and not always in the same direction. With three separate classical revivals (Louis Quatorze, Louis Seize and Napoleon III), two asymmetrical movements inspired by nature (Rococo and Art

Nouveau) and at least two stages where simplicity and craftsmanship replaced showmanship (Directoire and Art Deco), the Paris interior, as design historian Peter Thornton has aptly observed, is like 'a twisting, meandering river that has at various times backed up on itself'. And what is left today is obviously worth keeping.

Perhaps as compelling as what has survived is what has not. Despite the vast resources that Louis XIV threw at the decorative arts – and the fact that he was reponsible for placing France firmly at the top of the style hierarchy – the Louis Quatorze style plays little part in today's Paris interior. Louis Quatorze furniture is too heavy, too Baroque, for the typical Parisian apartment. Napoleon's Empire style suffered the same historical fate. Despite Bonaparte's monumental achievement in putting post-Revolutionary France back on its economic feet, his style is not particularly popular today. Even though it was much copied in its time, today's Parisian considers it too much the style of bureaucracy, suited to a civil servant or a career diplomat at best. Moreover, as with Louis Quatorze, the style's colours (lots of bright purple and bright red) and material (shiny mahogany decorated with gold eagles, swans and bees) make it difficult to combine with another period or style.

The same goes for Art Deco. Such pieces are undeniably fine examples of craftsmanship and virtuosity but they present a problem when one attempts to combine them with items from other styles and eras. Deco was designed as a complete scheme: it does not mix.

The Paris interior is a rich and vibrant fusion that combines the collective contribution of historical precedent with the dynamism of a desire to be modern. All in all, it is the result of a tireless drive to find the best way of bringing together 'life' and 'art'.

LOUIS v LOUIS

During the mid-nineteenth century, less than 60 years after the French Revolution ended Louis XVI's reign with a spectacular bloodbath, the style of furniture named after the last Bourbon monarch was once again all the rage. This was largely a result of Empress Eugénie's fascination with Marie Antoinette and the fashions she inspired. It was the start of a seemingly never-ending merry-go-round of stylistic imitation that focused particularly on the chairs that belonged to the reigns of Louis XV and Louis XVI.

The popularity of these chairs is such that reproductions dating from the first half of the nineteenth century can be almost as sought after as the originals themselves. Many original Louis Quinze and Louis Seize pieces perished during the Revolution, and the scarce examples surviving from the eighteenth century are now so precious that they tend to be found only in the decorative arts wings of well-endowed museums such as the Getty, the Louvre or the V&A. They were, after all, the work of artisans who took furniture-making to a level of artistry that had never before, and has

certainly never since, been taken to such limits. In an age where almost everything is mass produced, it is difficult to imagine that a piece of furniture such as Louis XV's *bureau du roi* took a team of dedicated craftsmen seven years to complete (the *bureau* was begun by Jean-François Oeben, cabinetmaker to the king, and completed by his successor, Jean-Henri Riesener). It was a period when furniture manufacturing was briefly elevated to the status of high art. But ironically, although an exquisite execution of detail is what set apart the furniture made for Louis XV and XVI, it is the shapes and forms that survive and continue to be imitated today, rather than the quality of the craftsmanship.

A revival of a 'style' tends to be regarded as a nineteenth-century phenomenon that grew out of a romantic interest in the past, but there is more to the enduring success of Louis Quinze and Louis Seize chairs than mere nostalgia for the grace and luxury of the French court in the

eighteenth century. These chairs were very well designed because the French aristocrats who commissioned them were extremely demanding, capricious and pedantic customers. Louis Quinze and Louis Seize chairs were far more practical than we might assume. Qualities such as scale, size and comfort were endlessly considered by these difficult but knowledgeable patrons – though Madame Victoire, daughter of Louis XV, was obviously a satisfied customer when she declared, '*Voici un fauteuil qui me perd*' ('Here is a chair in which I can lose myself'). With little else to do, the eighteenth-century nobility examined the merits of a chair with a seriousness that people today would apply to their choice of car.

Louis XV's predecessor, Louis XIV (the 'Sun King'), had presided over a court that aspired to new heights of grandeur, opulence, luxury and comfort. When he died in 1715 the crown went to his great-grandson, then a five-year-old child. Almost immediately there was a marked shift in attitude, and by the time Louis XV was crowned in 1723 (following

the death of the regent, Philippe, Duc d'Orléans) the French upper classes were no longer so wealthy. (Trying to compete with the king had all but cleaned them out.) In an effort to hang on to their hereditary estates and titles, marriages of convenience to daughters of rich but bourgeois bankers and speculators became commonplace. Commerce had married into life at court; the Roi du Soleil would have been horrified. It was a time of great corruption – licentiousness and intrigue had replaced pomp and formality – and ministers of state began to use their influence to make money for themselves. The great state receptions that marked Louis XVI's reign gave way to a society in which the boudoir became more important. This trend was reflected in fashions for furniture. Everything became smaller, more fanciful and more romantic. Screens and panels were decorated with paintings of love scenes and representations of ladies and gentlemen who look as though they must pass their entire existence in the elaboration of their toilettes and the exchange of compliments and pleasantries.

The *guéridon*, a small round occasional table; the *encoignure*, or corner cabinet; the *bonheur du jour*, a small desk; and the *fauteuil*, an armchair with upholstered rather than open sides, were all invented to suit smaller and more effeminate apartments. Even the design of the celebrated Gobelins tapestries – used for covering the finest furniture – changed. The bold, vigorous hunting scenes that were the height of fashion in Louis XIV's time gave way to shepherds, nymphs and exotic birds and animals.

working on the expensive pieces (*meubles de luxe*), 14,500 on the cheaper *meubles courants* and another 500 *trôleurs* to wheel the pieces round to the retailers.

Officially the Louis Quinze 'revival' was at its height from 1830 to 1930, but it is doubtful that these 250-year-old designs ever really went out of fashion ... and certainly not in Paris.

The Louis Seize style has enjoyed a similarly enduring success. Even before Louis XV's death in 1774, the prevailing fashion in design and architecture was beginning to change. As a result of the discoveries of Pompeii and Herculaneum and in response to a certain aristocratic 'fatigue' with organic individualism, straight lines started to replace broken scrolls, and columns reappeared in building facades. Interior decoration followed suit. Furniture was being streamlined in line with this new fashion for Neo-classicism – but the sizes and proportions remained the same. For this reason people often confuse Louis Quinze and Louis Seize chairs. But it is actually quite easy to distinguish between them: Louis Quinze legs are curved, while those on Louis Seize chairs are straight and tapered.

Towards the mid-nineteenth century – almost a hundred years after the Louis Quinze style had first flourished – the growing society of the 'well-to-do' in France decided it wanted a return to that comfortable and indulgent lifestyle. The old taste became the 'new taste'. Almost identical copies of eighteenth-century originals were commonly ordered as a suite – consisting of a *canapé*, two *fauteuils* and four side chairs. A look at the size of the furniture industry in Paris during the late nineteenth century gives some idea of how many of these suites were being made. Around 17,000 workers were employed in what was then the undisputed centre of furniture production in Europe, with 2,000

And so it transpires that, despite the upheavals of the Revolution, and despite the fact that France today is one of the most technologically advanced nations in the world, possibly the most successful pieces in the entire history of furniture design are the chairs favoured by the last two absolute monarchs of France. In fact, it is almost impossible to conceive of a stylish Paris interior without its Louis Quinze or Louis Seize chairs: whether upholstered with tapestry or plain silk, they can be found in almost every grand hotel or chic apartment.

Towards the end of the nineteenth century London's Victoria & Albert Museum was bequeathed the John Jones Collection, an important assembly of French furniture. A contemporary article in *The Times* newspaper surveyed these gems of eighteenth- and early nineteenth-century French workmanship and attempted to explain the historic and artistic value of the legacy. An excerpt from that article can provide a fitting conclusion to this chapter: 'As the visitor passes by the cases where these curious objects are

displayed, he asks himself – what is to be said on behalf of the art of which they are such notable examples? These tables, chairs, commodes, secretaires, wardrobes etc. represent in a singularly complete way the work of the *ancien régime* ... They bring back to us the grace, the luxury, the prettiness, the frivolity of that Court which believed itself, till the rude awakening came, to contain all that was precious in the life of France.' Those words sum up perfectly the ambience of that bygone age.

On a contemporary note, Louis Quinze and Louis Seize chairs are, in terms of sheer numbers being made and sold, more popular now than they were at the time of the Bourbon dynasty. More remarkably, they have kept their aristocratic bearing in a world where aristocracy no longer exists. Today, they are the chairs of choice for the finest restaurants, the most important dining rooms and the most celebrated homes. Louis Quinze and Louis Seize chairs are the result of one of those rare moments in history when something of outstanding beauty also happens to be practical and well designed.

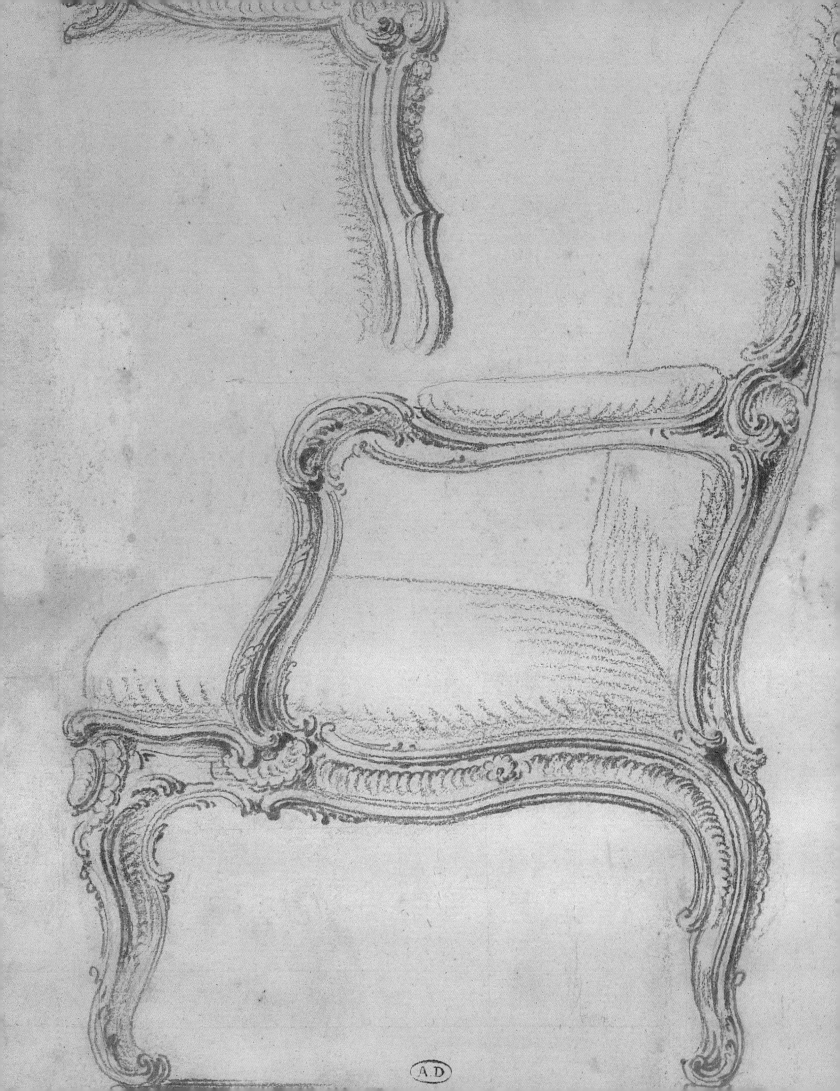

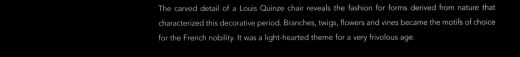

The carved detail of a Louis Quinze chair reveals the fashion for forms derived from nature that characterized this decorative period. Branches, twigs, flowers and vines became the motifs of choice for the French nobility. It was a light-hearted theme for a very frivolous age.

Louis Seize chairs (or more accurately reproduction Louis Seize) are once more highly fashionable, upholstered in the plain-coloured silks once favoured by Marie Antoinette. She and her husband Louis XVI preferred furniture with straight legs and classical fluting rather than the curved legs that distinguish the style of Louis Quinze.

Marlene Dietrich was a big fan of Paris – in terms of Parisian interiors her taste, perhaps not surprisingly, ran along the lines of Marie Antoinette's. She adored soft shades of mauve, lilac and pink and had a weakness for delicate objects, preferably decorated in the chinoiserie style.

Pale, soft and feminine, the Louis Seize style features straight lines and classical detailing – a reaction to the curling, scrolling excesses of the Rococo. It was the minimalism of its day, and as such appeals very much to contemporary sensibilities.

A daybed, an Aubusson rug (by the late eighteenth century Aubusson had started to specialize very successfully in tapestries for the floor), a collection of upright Louis Seize chairs and a subtle boiserie are contemporary testament to the enduring stylistic legacy of the Louis Seize period. The sophisticated pale colours are typical of the late eighteenth century.

Louis XVI (1754–93) is depicted here in the colours of the Bourbon dynasty: white and gold. More interested in hunting and making locks than in ruling the country, he was nonetheless a well-meaning monarch who was prepared to compromise. It was, however, a case of too little too late.

Louis XV (1710–74), the longest-ruling of all the Bourbon Louis, was an individual of great vitality. He was also a ladies' man with more than a passing interest in fashion and design: with his leopardskin sleeve he has the unmistakable air of an eighteenth-century dandy.

Louis XIV (1638–1715), the 'Sun King', managed to outlive his own son and grandsons; upon his death the crown passed to his great-grandson. By the time Louis XV was old enough to take the throne in 1723, the French aristocracy had abandoned the great pomp of Versailles and the fashion was for small, comfortable apartments. The *fauteuil*, an armchair whose sides are filled in with upholstery, was an invention of the time. It is shown here in two colours.

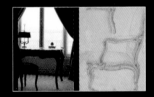

The reason Louis Quinze and Louis Seize pieces often get confused is that they are similar in terms of size and scale. The decorative approach changed with the advent of Neo-classicism, as seen here, but not the basic shape or proportion.

The Neo-classical Louis Seize style actually emerged before Louis XVI became king. Louis XV, however, remained faithful to the end to the more curvaceous Rococo style. Furniture with straight legs had no place in any of Louis XV's palace apartments.

On his rounds of official duties at Versailles, Louis XIV would often stop and admire his paintings – particularly the ones of himself. Not only did the Sun King identify strongly with the Roman Empire (hence the many paintings of him seated on a horse and wearing a toga, Caesar-style) but he also saw his palace at Versailles as the residence of the king in the way that Mount Olympus was the residence of the Greek gods. This painting by Jean Nocret, from 1670, depicts the king and his entire family disposed like gods in a setting straight out of mythology.

CHINOISERIE

Throughout history, China has for the West represented the mysterious, magical unknown, the epitome of exoticism. Goods from China have captured imaginations ever since Chinese silk first made its way along the caravan routes to be eagerly traded with the Romans, who were fascinated by this 'lustrous cloth'. They did not know how this delicate fabric was made, nor did they know anything about the land it was made in. All they knew was that it came from far, far away, which surely made Chinese silk even more desirable.

Demand may have been high but trade with China was difficult, and became increasingly so with the rise of Islam. By the year 878 the 'Silk Route' through Central Asia to Europe had ceased to be viable: China closed its doors to foreigners, and became an inviolable and secret country that was to remain that way for centuries. The land that Marco Polo would describe as being at 'the ends of the earth' was now even more mysterious. Only the odd visitor – among them Friar Odoric in the 1300s and Matteo Ricci in the early

seventeenth century, as well as Marco Polo himself in the thirteenth century – was allowed a peek inside the magic kingdom of Cathay. These travellers' accounts of what they saw became not only bestselling books, translated into myriad languages, but also Europe's only reference to life in the mysterious East. It was an imperfect and romanticized understanding, which provided fertile ground for the development of chinoiserie.

By the time the Portuguese finally got a foot in the door, in the sixteenth century, with a small trading post in the port of Macao, Europe was convinced that China was a land overflowing with precious gems, spices and silks: a place where people whiled away the hours in bamboo pavilions perched on idyllic points overlooking picturesque winding rivers, a land typified by descriptions of Kublai Khan's sumptuous palace at Xanadu, with only the odd drawback of 'man-eating lizards' (alligators). Even if more accurate accounts existed (and they did), it was the romantic notion of

China – the 'myth of Cathay' – that captured the public's imagination. Moreover, the shiploads of silk, ivory, lacquer and porcelain that began arriving from the East were for most people evidence enough that China really was a land of untold splendour.

As a result of Portugal's monopoly in China, Lisbon was soon one of the richest cities in Europe. Eager to receive their share of these spoils, both Holland and England, and later Sweden and France, founded companies for trade in the Far East. By the time France got in on the act in the late 1600s – the last European nation to do so – Holland had already imported well over three million pieces of blue-and-white porcelain. As could perhaps be expected with Louis XIV on the throne, however, it was not long before the French had begun to outstrip their rivals and dominate the Eastern trade, particularly as regards matters of taste and style.

The Sun King's approach to chinoiserie could hardly be deemed half-hearted. Through his Compagnie des Indes he was able to fill Versailles with lacquer and porcelain on a vast scale. Chinoiserie got the royal *imprimatur*, and the other courts in Europe duly followed suit. The Sun King, as was his wont, went one step further by building the Trianon de Porcelaine, a group of three single-storey pavilions in the grounds of Versailles, decorated inside and out with chinoiserie. It was intended as a 'love shack' for the king and his mistress the Marquise de Montespan but unfortunately the roof – made entirely of blue-and-white porcelain tiles – leaked like a sieve, and the whole *folie* did not last more than a couple of decades. In any case, Louis XIV was by then romantically linked with with the more pious Madame de Maintenon, who was unlikely to have appreciated its exotic connotations. Nevertheless, a trend had been set. Other princes, kings and electors rushed off to build their own Chinese-style pavilions – such as the Pagodenburg built at Nymphenburg by Max Emmanuel, elector of Bavaria; or the Japanisches Palais in Dresden constructed by August the Strong, King of Poland and Elector of Saxony.

By the late 1600s Europe was in the grip of a mania for all things Chinese: embroidered silk panels, lacquered screens and cabinets, golden filigree ... the *beau monde* could not get enough. Demand far outstripped supply, and European craftsmen attempted to fill the gap with local imitations. Colbert, Louis XIV's 'Mr Fix It', instigated the production of *faïence* (tin-glazed earthenware) in imitation of Chinese porcelain at Rouen and Nevers, in direct competition with established

porcelain factories at Delft in Holland. In the 1670s the Nevers factory began producing the highly successful *bleu persan*, a reverse variant of traditional Chinese 'blue-on-white', in a range of traditional Ming Dynasty shapes. But while European attempts to imitate Chinese porcelain, lacquerwork and silks certainly changed the manner in which chinoiserie was expressed, nothing had so big an impact as the advent of the fashion for Rococo.

Chinoiserie and the Rococo, it seemed, were tailor made for each other. It was not just the successful meeting of East and West, it was also the merger of two decorative directions that shared a common provenance: neither was based on the classics. The bright colours and fantastical imagination of chinoiserie fitted extremely well with the scrolls and asymmetrical, irregular ornament of the Rococo. And both styles had at their heart a paradox: they were childishly simple and yet intricately complex, with a playfulness that was somewhat at odds with their sophisticated environment. Louis XV, although still a child when the fashion for chinoiserie began, was an ardent supporter of the style, as was his wife (and his mistress). Such was Louis XV's passion for *ouvrages de la Chine* that the official inventory of the Crown had to produce a separate catalogue for his chinoiserie collection. Marie Antoinette, too, became a big fan. When she first arrived at Versailles, a young girl of 14 barely able to speak the language and betrothed to the future king of France, she was, understandably, fairly miserable. To cheer her up, her mother Maria Theresa, Empress of Austria, would send her little gilded Japanese dogs to remind her of the fondness for chinoiserie at Schönbrunn, the palace of her childhood. Later she

would grow up to become a serious collector of intricate and expensive pieces of lacquer furniture, setting the fashion not just for contemporary French society but for many subsequent generations.

At the time of Louis XIV, the image of China as depicted in fabrics and on murals was either grotesque or bizarre, or both. But with the advent of the more feminine, intimate and comfortable Rococo style, chinoiserie had become more sophisticated; the 'Chinese' people depicted in scenes by eighteenth-century artists such as Antoine Watteau and François Boucher had become recognizably Parisian. Boucher, in particular, introduced an appealing sensuality to what were essentially exotic versions of robust Arcadian scenes. His famous painting *The Chinese Fishing Party* of 1742, which would later be used for one of a series of tapestries entitled 'Tentures chinoises', set a fashion for scenes depicting attractive, languid Orientals in settings that were not so different from France – apart from the odd pagoda and a few stylized

umbrellas. The spirit of these creations was not lost on the nineteenth-century critics the Goncourt brothers, who observed: '*Approchez-vous! La Chinoise et le Seigneur qui prennent le Thé, ce sont des Parisiens*' ('Come closer! The Chinese lady and the elderly gent who are having Tea, they are Parisians'). Boucher's sensuous chinoiserie engravings were ultimately copied onto plates, panels, doors, snuffboxes and porcelain. So, too, was the work of Jean-Baptiste Pillement, who concentrated more on the fun and the fantasy of the East. He created a fanciful chinoiserie world where figures danced before a backdrop of Chinese-style birds, bridges and buildings; his rich compendium of light-hearted designs was perfectly suited to decorative murals and fabric, especially the increasingly popular *toiles de Jouy*.

By now any attempt at an accurate depiction of China had long been abandoned. As a style, chinoiserie thrived on allusion and reinterpretation: accuracy was neither important nor desirable

Chinoiserie had emerged as a strong decorative strain in its own right, and it had become the height of fashion. In 1720 one of the leading Parisian art dealers, Gersaint, a supplier to the king and all the top nobility, even changed the name of his shop from 'Au Grand Monarque' to 'A la Pagode'. Perhaps the ultimate example of the extent to which chinoiserie had become a self-contained style, however, is the fact that in the late 1700s Louis XV was bold enough to send a set of Boucher's 'Tentures chinoises' to the Chinese emperor, Chi'en Lung. The emperor pronounced himself delighted with them because they were so novel – and so French. (One was still hanging in the Imperial Palace when it was sacked by the British in 1860.)

A style of the imagination, conjured out of fantastic visions of the East, chinoiserie in France has never entirely been discarded. Like most French decorative styles it was revived during the second half of the nineteenth century. Subsequently, towards the turn of the century, the fashion for the Orient emerged in a new form as japonisme, a style concerned with, but not exactly imitating, the arts of Japan.

Even the advent of modernism in the twentieth century injected new life into chinoiserie: given a modern dress it was employed for high-profile projects such as the interiors of the great transatlantic liners. The Art Deco of the 1920s and 30s, like many French decorative styles, embodied a fascination with the new and an appreciation of individual craftsmanship. As a movement it was able simultaneously to embrace the modernism of Le Corbusier (1887–1965)

and the decadent luxury of Jacques-Emile Ruhlmann (1879–1933). Lacquer, or 'japanning', played an important role in Art Deco, and once again the two greatest exponents of the new style were both in Paris. Eileen Gray (1878–1976) and Jean Dunand (1877–1942) were the Boulle and the Riesener of their day. Like their *ancien régime* predecessors, they set new examples for the world to copy: lacquer was reinvented in a modern way. Once again, something Oriental was reinterpreted to become something very French. Art Deco lacquer combined the French love of *luxe* with the exoticism and colour of the East.

Historically speaking, it was a familiar formula. The creative credit goes to Eileen Gray, a young Scottish painter who had recently arrived in Paris from London. Trained as a restorer of old lacquer, she was apprenticed in Paris with a Japanese lacquer master, Sugawara. Patronized by couturier Jacques Doucet and others, she used costly traditional techniques in a modern idiom: a plain, deep red lacquer screen, for instance, would be decorated with Symbolist figures or abstract designs. Jean Dunand, originally a sculptor, also worked in this contemporary style. He added a new dimension by incorporating crushed eggshell to create a tactile, uneven surface – a technique that was even copied by some of the great Japanese lacquer masters.

Today, the exotic East remains as popular as ever. Chinoiserie not only survives in the context of eagerly collected antiques but also thrives in new expressions. In the words of one fashion magazine: 'Paris has gone mad for the Orient – again'. It seems that the spirit of 'L'Ouest meets l'Est' is sweeping the French capital. Gardens borrowing from Chinese refinement and from Japanese minimalism, such as the Jardins Albert Kahn or the Hôtel Heidelbach's Galeries du panthéon bouddique (which feature no fewer than one hundred Buddhas alongside a Japanese garden), seem to be all the rage, while Thai silks in Marie Antoinette-style colours such as plum and pale pink are the height of fashion for minimal, modern furniture. Joyce Ma's gallery in Paris, described as 'a window onto Asia', offers an unpredictable array of pieces with an Asian sensibility: yoga mats filled with silicone gel by Italian artist Luisa Cevese Riedizioni; calligraphy tableaux by Fabienne Verdier, the first European woman to be trained by master Chinese calligraphers; and rugs by American artists Brad Davis and Jane Provisor, woven with wild silk harvested in northern China. Restaurants serving 'fusion food', meanwhile, are equally fashionable in the French capital, and Franco–Japanese dishes such as Foie Gras Sushi with Sansho Pepper have got Paris in a spin. This, surely, is the heart of the 'new chinoiserie': the myth of Cathay lives on.

Chinoiserie, the romanticized interpretation of the mystical, exotic land of Cathay, afforded the craftsmen of the eighteenth and nineteenth centuries a rich source of decorative themes. Skills of draughtsmanship, gilding and lacquering were combined in the decoratation of all sorts of furniture; this detail shows a small occasional table. As with most pieces originating in the time of Louis XV, lacquer chinoiserie continued to be popular throughout the nineteenth century and particularly during the Second Empire (under Napoleon III), when anything Oriental was very much in fashion.

Since the eighteenth century there has rarely been a time when chinoiserie has not been in vogue in France. Coco Chanel, who revolutionized women's fashion with her modern, simplified outfits, was a big fan. The much-photographed salon of her private apartment in the Ritz was dominated by superb lacquered Chinese panels of the kind that were first popular in the time of Louis XV.

The depth and lustre of Chinese lacquer captured the imagination of the European aristocracy when it was first imported from the East. The demand was such that local craftsmen invested much time and energy in an effort to imitate it. The French Martin brothers were ultimately most successful in inventing something that most closely resembled the Chinese original. *Vernis Martin* soon became the accepted term in French for this highly sought-after finish.

Alongside lacquerware, porcelain was the other Chinese import that fascinated the European aristocracy. The makers of clay pottery were unable to duplicate its translucency and its combination of delicacy and durability. Porcelain was rare and eagerly collected, and special cabinets were commissioned to display these expensive trophies. Eventually the price came down – due to the sheer volume of pieces imported and the discovery of the secret of its manufacture – but by this time the china cabinet was firmly established as an important part of a noteworthy interior.

Chinese calligraphy and ink drawings on parchment scrolls reached Europe at the same time as lacquer and porcelain. They became particularly popular during the nineteenth-century Belle Epoque, when all things Oriental were thrown together in an effort to make a room as exotic as possible. Shown here is a twentieth-century example in the same idiom.

A contemporary Parisian dining room is decorated with a Chinese brush painting by the twentieth-century French artist Aurore de la Morinerier. Juxtaposed with a scatter cushion in red raw silk, it represents a modern interpretation of chinoiserie – a reflection of Parisians' enduring fascination with the culture of China.

The fine brushstrokes in ink – depicting a Chinese courtesan – on a background of coarsely textured paper belie the fact that this work was created by a contemporary French artist. It could quite easily be confused with an old Chinese scroll painting.

Not only did the Martin brothers invent a finish that closely resembled Chinese lacquer but they also introduced colours that were in step with the fashion of the day, such as lilacs, pinks and elegant shades of green. This new colour scheme also affected pottery and porcelain: traditional blue and white was all but abandoned in favour of a more sophisticated palette. In terms of pottery, decoration and colour became very French but the Chinese shape remained unchanged.

As soon as porcelain started arriving in Europe in the 1500s, as a result of Portugal's newly established trade with China, it became seriously coveted by European royalty and aristocracy. Initially the cost of collecting meant it was restricted to the privileged elite.

The distinctly shaped Chinese stool made of porcelain with a hollow interior became a popular mainstay of the Oriental taste of the Belle Epoque. In China these stools were designed to be placed on top of a small pile of hot coals; the heat would radiate through the porcelain while the holes allowed air to get to the coals to keep them burning. When transported into another culture this functional item became a purely decorative piece.

A concern for authenticity is the hallmark of modern-day chinoiserie. In contrast to the rampant fantasy of eighteenth-century creations, historical and cultural accuracy is now much sought after. Nonetheless, the whimsy of the antique and the authenticity of today mix well together.

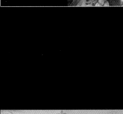

Painting has played an important role in chinoiserie ever since the eighteenth-century artist François Boucher amused the French aristocracy with his tableaux that essentially placed upper-class Parisians in vaguely Chinese Arcadian scenes. The abundant, exotic riches of Cathay were a popular theme. The Russian emigré artist Boris Pastoukhoff – like Mark Chagall, another talented White Russian – painted this still-life with Chinese figures in the late 1920s and left it in a hotel to pay his bill.

At the height of the eighteenth century's obsession with chinoiserie, the playful Chinese figures created by artist Jean-Baptiste Pillement became a popular favourite – especially when printed on *toile de Jouy* as shown here. In contrast to François Boucher's more sophisticated depictions of chinoiserie themes, there was a lightness and sense of fun to Pillement's work that helped establish a genre of chinoiserie *toile de Jouy* that is still in demand today. Nowadays, however, far fewer choices exist than at the time when Monsieur Oberkampf's factory was catering to customers such as Marie Antoinette and Madame de Pompadour.

The last of the Rococo chinoiserie designers was also the most fun. Jean-Baptiste Pillement's creations were pure fairyland, and the lively little people who populated his drawings gave rise to a form of expression now referred to as the 'Pillement style'. At the same time as Pillement's spirited creations were the height of fashion on fabric, his style of design was also used to adorn lacquered furniture. Indeed, Rococo chinoiserie furniture was nothing to do with real Chinese furniture. It was only *chinois* in colour (red and black), and in small amounts of decorative detail. Even at the height of the vogue for chinoiserie, this detail was applied with orderly restraint.

François Boucher, Madame de Pompadour's favourite artist, created his own genre of painting in the chinoiserie style. The myth of Cathay, originally mysterious and sometimes foreboding, became in his hands something charming, erotic even. In the decadent court of Louis XV it was, understandably, a big hit. Boucher's work was widely imitated and his own creations – such as this one – were applied in myriad ways, including a set of tapestries called 'Teintures chinoises' made in the workshops of Beauvais. So enamoured was Louis XV with these tapestries that he gave a set to the Chinese

OBJETS TROUVÉS

It has been said that each period of French history has contributed something to the collective total that we now recognize as the Paris interior. If this is true, then the nineteenth century's most valuable contribution has no doubt been the notion of eclecticism: the successful combination of decorative pieces that were not designed to go together.

In pre-Revolutionary France, the basic premise as far as design and decoration were concerned was that to be fashionable (and being fashionable was *de rigeur*) all objects had to reflect the same constellation of physical attributes: similar forms, motifs, patterns and shapes. But the nineteenth century changed all that. To a wealthy bourgeoisie obsessed with the past glories of French design, every decorative style – from the Renaissance to Louis Quatorze, Louis Quinze and Louis Seize – was ripe for picking in the search for more opulence and more luxury. French retailers (who played an increasingly dominant role in furnishing the bourgeois Parisian apartment) served to accelerate the development of this

eclecticism by offering pieces that incorporated features taken from the entire lexicon of French decorative history. What had been lost in purity had been gained in diversity and choice, and these goods now had to appeal to a much larger audience.

From 1852 to 1870, the period of the Second Empire under Napoleon III (1808–73), France enjoyed what has often been referred to as a second renaissance. Once again the French decorative arts dominated the world marketplace. This time, however, the French dominance of taste and style was based on a solid foundation of well-established luxury industries rather than the overspending of an indulged monarch and his court. Companies such as Hermès (leather, founded 1837), Christofle (silver, founded 1830), Baccarat (crystal, founded 1828) and Sèvres (porcelain, relaunched by Napoleon in the early 1800s) enjoyed the eager patronage of an affluent middle class as well as increasing demand from abroad (particularly the United States, where everything French was very

much in vogue) – which produced valuable export earnings. Although it was a renaissance centred on the middle classes, the lessons of the *ancien régime* – excellence of craftsmanship, quality of materials and fine attention to detail – were not lost on this increasingly affluent and demanding group of consumers. One of the results was the revival of the Louis Seize style at this time. The fact that Empress Eugénie (wife of Napoleon III) was a big fan of Marie Antoinette, and of her 'markedly developed sensibility', of course helped, but the underlying Louis Seize principles of proportion, scale and quality were the cornerstones of the style's revival. Nobody, of course, could afford to spend on exquisite detail as the Bourbon kings had done, but there was only a slight decline in the exquisiteness of the craftsmanship. The real difference, of course, lay in the way these various reproductions were used. For example, a typical well-to-do Parisian apartment of the late nineteenth century might have a *petit salon* largely furnished in the Louis Seize reproduction style, alongside a *salon* or reception room in a heavier, more formal, reproduction Louis Quatorze.

Inevitably this trend for revivals led to a distinction between 'antique' and 'reproduction'. Thus there arose, towards the latter part of the nineteenth century, the connotations that we today associate with the

word 'antique'. A chair, table or candlestick that was actually from the period of revival acquired a special value. Prior to the revival-prone Second Empire, an old object was exactly that: old. In an environment of accumulation and nostalgia, however, antiques became valuable commodities that were much sought after. The fashion for revivals added another facet to the Parisian interior, and one that has continued to this day, namely the display of a special object or piece that does not necessarily share historical or stylistic consistency with its surroundings.

Of course, collecting per se was not a French invention: the ancient Greeks collected Oriental carpets, the Romans coveted Indian and Chinese silks, and during the Renaissance whole rooms were given over to 'cabinets of curiosities'. But the French can be credited with redefining and broadening the scope of what could be considered collectable, by adding the idea that pieces from one's own relatively recent cultural past were suitable. Collecting henceforth became mass-market and nationalistic.

The twentieth century, with its emphasis on individualism, added the twist that objects need not be beautiful in the classical sense, nor even valuable by traditional standards (nor, for that matter, need they be

antique). In France, perhaps following a precedent set by Marie Antoinette with her taste for the unusual, collecting manifested itself in the cult of the *objet trouvé*.

Today a Parisian interior is almost inconceivable without the character, charm and surprise of the found object. The vast size of the Paris flea market at Porte de Clignancourt, for example, is testament to the enduring appeal of the old, the odd and the eccentric. It might be a vintage Hermès silk scarf used to upholster a footstool, a scruffy nineteenth-century leopardskin, a collection of Paris Exposition postcards circa 1900 or an early twentieth-century Pernod poster. When it comes to *objets trouvés* there are no rules: the less predictable and more inventive, the better.

Found objects can take on a whole new meaning within a contemporary environment. The lamps featured in this chapter are a good example. Originally they were oversized perfume bottles, made

in the the early 1900s for display in pharmacies and *parfumeries*. The idea of turning them into lamps is typical of the way imagination and creativity can transform the found object. Indeed, the manner in which an *objet trouvé* is used is almost as important as the object itself – if not more so. A bridle, for instance, no matter how beautifully made, would seem an odd thing to hang on a wall unless – as in a noted Parisian *hôtel particulier* – the walls happen to be those of a former *porte cochère*, where the reference to horses is historically potent. And therein lies the power of even the most obscure or unusual object. French history has such depth and diversity that in France it is difficult to find an object that does not have some story to tell.

Andrée Putman, one of France's most successful and influential late twentieth-century designers, once said in an interview that when she judges an interior in terms of style she looks for the mistake – for the bizarre element. No mistake ... no style: perhaps that is the best definition of the role of the *objet trouvé* in today's Paris interior.

At one time almost every formal dining room in France had a pair of *girandoles* such as this sitting on a sideboard – which is why they can still be found at most Parisian flea markets. Originally illuminated with candles, they are still captivating even using electric light. Famous crystal glass manufacturers such as Daum, Baccarat and Cristalleries de Saint-Louis, established during the first half of the nineteenth century, used their uniquely French approach of hand-making in volume to cater to the demands of the newly emerging middle class.

These elegant and unusual lamps started life as merchandising material. Made in the early 1900s – complete with cut-glass stoppers – to display perfume, they are a perfect example of a 'found object' being imaginatively reinterpreted as a decorative centrepiece. The addition of dyed water sets these pear-shaped decanters apart.

Tables, chairs, paintings, screens ... an *objet trouvé* is not limited to any one particular genre. It can be anything – preferably something unexpected – that gives a room a sense of personality and individuality. Historically, the French love of the unusual goes back to the vogue for *cabinets de curiosités* at a time when members of the aristocracy shared a penchant for collecting strange and unusual objects.

Small screens, particularly those with glazed panels, were traditionally used in Parisian interiors to add light and decorative detail to a room.

Another oversized perfume display bottle, this time from Guerlain, 1920s; not just a beautiful object, it also highlights the importance of perfume throughout French history. Exquisite perfume bottles of cut crystal were first introduced to France by Catherine de' Medici, wife of Henri II, and by the time Louis XIV was on the throne, perfume was a major industry in France. Glassmakers, goldsmiths and other artisans helped produce an extraordinary array of stunning scent bottles. Louis XIV had his own perfume, called *Martial,* and perfume was used with such abandon during the reign of Louis XV that his entourage was referred to as *la cour parfumée* ('the perfumed court'). Marie Antoinette had her favourite fragrances – violet and rose – and Napoleon, not to be outdone by the *ancien régime,* went through two quarts of *eau de cologne* a week.

A bust in the Roman model was for a long time one of the basic decorative ingredients of a French interior. Until it was replaced by the clock, it took pride of place in the centre of the mantelpiece, with candelabra in ormolu (mercury-gilded bronze) placed on either side. Today plaster has largely replaced carved marble and mercury gilding is no longer possible because of the health risks, but both the bust and the candelabra endure as favourite decorative elements.

Fer forgé, or wrought iron, is another example of craftsmanship in which the French have historically excelled, as a look at the balconies of many Parisian apartments will testify. In this case a Rococo console table base has been regilded and fitted with a new marble top. Pieces of *fer forgé* – from radiator covers to stair banisters – can be found in great variety in Parisian flea markets.

The Louis Quinze style is generally identified with an abundance of asymmetrically arranged natural motifs. However, the use of classical imagery was so deeply ingrained in French culture – as a result of the efforts of Louis XIV – that motifs such as bronze faces and busts were never completely abandoned. Instead, they were streamlined and adapted to the new style – which, in a sense, is a metaphor for the entire history of the French decorative arts.

A wall-mounted candle sconce in gilded bronze is pure Rococo in style, taking its decorative cue from nature (particularly leaves). The other distinctive mark is its use of what is known as the 'S' curve which, together with the 'C' curve, constitutes the main decorative vocabulary of the Rococo. As with most Louis Quinze-style pieces found today, this wall sconce dates from the late 1800s/early 1900s, a time when Paris produced a huge number of reproduction pieces.

The literal definition of the French word '*boiserie*' is simply 'wooden panelling'. In the context of the history of the French decorative arts, however, its importance cannot be overestimated. It is impossible to imagine an interior from the any of grandest periods of French history without rooms decorated with boiseries. Simply by covering walls in carved and embellished timber, the French invented a means of conveying formality, grandeur, delicacy and, in later years, intimacy. Yet boiserie was rarely as simple as it might appear. Its success, whether it was used in a grand formal reception room or an intimate *cabinet*, depended on a strong and informed feeling for scale and proportion. There is a sophisticated sense of geometry at work in panelled rooms, which is derived from the legacy of the *ancien régime*.

All of which, as is usually the case with the French decorative arts, brings us back to Louis XIV (1638–1715). With his more than adequate ego, the Sun King was concerned – if not obsessed – with leaving his mark for future generations. An attentive student of history, he was particularly interested in Ancient Rome and the Italian Renaissance, and encouraged his architects to use Classical and Renaissance models and principles as the starting point for their designs. The Romans did not use timber panelling but they did divide their walls into 'fields', where the upper portion was decorated with murals and the lower part (delineated by what we now call a dado) was kept in a plain but coordinating colour. The Italian Renaissance improved upon this formula with the introduction of frescoes, particularly on the upper field.

Louis XIV, together with his First Painter Charles Le Brun (1619–90) and his team of artisans, took wall adornment one step further, introducing a three-dimensional element by way of intricate wooden panels.

In keeping with the grandeur and ornateness of the Baroque, Louis XIV insisted on combining a range of earlier historical styles of wall decoration. Thus, not only were the boiseries that adorned the state

rooms of Versailles and other palaces intricately and exquisitely carved but they also featured fields of extravagantly painted murals – often depicting heroic scenes of military conquests and tableaux from ancient mythology. Also in evidence were high mirrors, marble insets, trompe l'oeil effects and, of course, plenty of gilding. Even this orgy of excess was not without historical precedent: it closely resembles the grotesques (wall paintings) of antiquity as depicted and imitated by Raphael (1483–1520) and Francesco Primaticcio (1504–70) and indeed it is thought to have been modelled upon those artists' decorative schemes.

arrangement with an oval medallion featuring a classical bust – a composition not unlike a vibrant three-dimensional scrapbook of historical motifs. And this was only one part of one room.

But it is doubtful whether boiserie would have had such an enduring impact if it had not been for developments during the reign of Louis XV, an epoch that witnessed a decorative backlash against the excesses of Louis XIV. The Sun King played a game that nobody could win. He encouraged and indeed initiated lavish spending on outward appearances – in fashion, architecture, decoration and landscape design – in which his nobles were meant to

During the reign of Louis XIV, wall design, especially boiserie, was considered to be part of the furniture. The work of Jean Le Pautre (1618–82), one of the king's favourite artisans, was typical of the splendid monumentality the Roi du Soleil aspired to. Above one of his console tables – adorned with carved legs depicting mythological figures and with carved garlands draped along the front – Le Pautre would typically place a mirror framed by the same decorative garlands that decorated the console. To this he would add numerous gilded putti (cherubs) and then crown the whole

participate. The end result – after Louis XIV and those around him had indulged in ever more excessive expenditure for the better part of five decades – was that by the time of the king's death, the French aristocracy was on the verge of ruin. Politically, this prodigal overspending was one of Louis XIV's shrewdest moves: no member of French nobility had any resources left with which to raise an army to challenge him, and France, as a nation, benefited from an outward display of wealth which no other European country could match.

After the Sun King's death, the Regency provided a much-needed break for French aristocracy from the competitive extravagance of Versailles. Tired of the relentless pomp and formality of the court, and chastized by empty coffers, many of the nobility started to move their main residences back to Paris where they sought a more relaxed lifestyle and rediscovered an enthusiasm for entertaining. Accordingly, the architectural emphasis shifted from the monumental state rooms of Louis

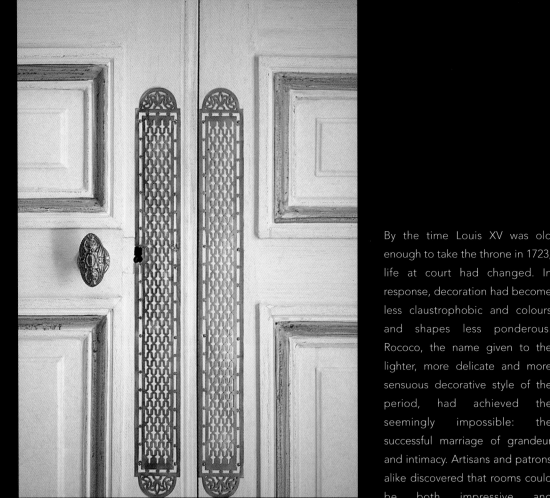

By the time Louis XV was old enough to take the throne in 1723, life at court had changed. In response, decoration had become less claustrophobic and colours and shapes less ponderous. Rococo, the name given to the lighter, more delicate and more sensuous decorative style of the period, had achieved the seemingly impossible: the successful marriage of grandeur and intimacy. Artisans and patrons alike discovered that rooms could be both impressive and

Boiserie played an important role during the Rococo era, as is evidenced by the quantity of documentation that has survived to this day. Thousands of sketches, plans and layouts for boiseries survive in historical archives all over France. Of particular importance is the work of Nicolas Pineau (1684–1754). His designs for wall and door panels, while using the standard vocabulary of 'S'- and 'C'-shaped scrolls, display great skill and inventiveness: even the most rudimentary of his sketches seems to contain the essence of the Parisian Rococo. Pineau was to become the most sought-after and fashionable designer of the period, and his much-acclaimed work on the Peterhof in St Petersburg sealed his reputation.

Parisian designers were in great demand all over Europe. Juste-Aurèle Meissonier (1695–1750), appointed Dessinateur de la Chambre et du Cabinet du Roi in 1726, also worked for other royal clients such as Count Bielenski, the Grand Marshall of Poland. Meanwhile, Gilles-Marie Oppenord (1672–1742), famous for his interior decoration of the Palais Royal in Paris, counted among his patrons Elector Clement-August of Cologne, producing work for him in Bonn, Brühl and Falkenlust.

Eventually, the exuberance of the Rococo became just too exuberant. Certain influential members of French nobility – notably Madame de Pompadour, Louis XV's mistress – began to look once more to the classics as a way of exercising some restraint. There followed a return to symmetry, proportion and straight lines – a style associated with Louis XVI although in fact the change had already begun before he took the throne. This return to classicism under the final years of the French monarchy had important repercussions for boiserie. Already reinvented during the reign of Louis XV, boiseries were now streamlined still further, resulting in a style that has timeless

appeal. The boiserie of Louis Seize retains the splendour, the intimacy and the accessibility of its predecessors, but adds to it a classic quality which makes it eminently suitable for interior furnishings of almost any style, past or present.

Filtered, stylistically, through the three most influential courts of the French monarchy, at a time when France – and especially Paris – was pre-eminent in matters of style and taste, it is no wonder that boiserie as it emerged in the late eighteenth century has retained its popularity through two centuries of history. It surely ranks as one of the most recognizable ingredients of what we today regard as the typical Paris interior.

The Belle Epoque, a period that corresponds to the rule of Napoleon III, was a time of economic resurgence, when the newly emerging Parisian middle class could afford to indulge in revivals of whatever French historical style took their fancy. These panelled doors embody a highly decorative mix that is typical of the late 1800s. They combine the classical imagery so loved by Louis XIV with the floral decoration of the Rococo, all rendered in the light, muted colours that are identified mainly with the Louis Seize style.

Although the style of Louis XIV is generally associated with Baroque excess, the basic rectangular form that is standard to almost all boiseries stems, nonetheless, from the time of the Sun King. It was Louis XIV who abandoned the use of tapestries on the wall in favour of carved wooden panelling. Although the extravagant panelling of Versailles is often seen as typical of this period, much French boiserie of the early 1700s was distinguished by its simplicity and sobriety.

Jacques-François Blondel, Professor of Architecture at the Louvre (whose famous students included Claude-Nicolas Ledoux, William Chambers and Robert Adam), created a manifesto on appropriate colours for boiseries. White, in his opinion, worked best for rooms destined to be used during the day, where its freshness would be appropriate. Colours such as jonquille and citron yellow, alongside pale blues and greens, were deemed more appropriate for smaller rooms. But the library and the billiard room, he specified, should be panelled in oak and varnished but never painted.

Perhaps the most significant contribution of the Rococo was its ability to combine cosiness and grandeur. A new way of decorating and detailing was introduced: rooms were clad with boiseries that by earlier royal standards would hardly have been considered decorated. Ornament became delicate; the impression was of lightness and femininity, and the overall appearance more natural than previously. No wonder, then, that this style has been revived so often and continues to influence the decorative choices of today.

There are almost no details or refinements in a Paris interior that do not have a historical precedent. Louis XIV began the fashion for using a contrasting colour to highlight the detailing of a panel. Today's interpretation of boiserie may be much simpler, but the practice of highlighting with a single colour persists. That is the strength of the Paris interior: all ideas, all content, have been tested by time; it has been an evolutionary, rather than a revolutionary, process.

Whereas the boiseries of Louis XIV were more often than not heavily adorned with *faux* finishes, insets of marble and painted scenes of manly pursuits such as the hunt, Rococo brought with it a thematic transformation. In keeping with the style's lightness and femininity, the subjects of painted panels (which had reduced substantially in size and in number) became noticeably less heroic and much more romantic.

One of the most remarkable differences between Parisian boiseries and the panelled rooms found in other European countries is the brilliant effect created in Paris by large plates of looking-glass. Under the patronage of Louis XIV, French workshops invented the means to make mirrors of a size that was certainly beyond the capacity of the Venetians who had previously dominated this field.

A sketch by court architect Nicolas Pineau, preserved in the archives of the Musée des Arts Decoratifs in Paris. Pineau was much in demand, particularly for his talent for creating boiserie schemes of extraordinary detail. Most of his work was commissioned for the royal palaces of Europe (at the time, Pineau was to interior architecture what Le Nôtre was to landscape gardens: a visionary). Boiserie was the essential framework of a successful interior: it was a decorative 'code' within which the architect placed the different elements at his disposal, such as paintings, clocks and furniture.

As with almost all matters concerning design or architecture, the concept of wall-to-wall panelling evolved from the Ancient Greeks and Romans. The proportions of French panelling were based on those of Corinthian, Ionian and Etruscan pillars. The division into 'fields', separated by a dado rail, stems from the Ancient Roman practice of decorating the upper half of an interior wall with murals and leaving the lower part plain. While today boiserie might be perceived as purely a decorative option, historically it was taken very seriously indeed. In eighteenth-century France, members of the aristocracy exchanged letters on the merits of panelling in the dining room, finding it more appropriate than fabric because it didn't absorb odours. The most accomplished French architects of the day (Blondel and Pineau among them) would not even consider becoming involved with an interior unless the client intended to specify boiseries for the majority, if not all, of the rooms.

Under the rule of Napoleon, France became a rich nation. The country had recovered from revolutionary anarchy and the French economy had produced a comfortably well-off bourgeoisie that, ironically, aspired to the style of the deposed *ancien régime*. The styles of the last three Bourbon kings were re-created in waves of neo-Quatorze, neo-Quinze and neo-Seize to such a extent that they confused tradesmen and designers alike; furniture historian Delvis Molesworth has referred to the phenomenon as '*le style tous les Louis*'.

A piece of Belle Epoque detailing is a good example, combining Louis Quatorze-style medallions and Louis Quinze garlands within an overall symmetry that recalls Louis Seize. The soft, muted colours of the bedroom as a whole are typical of the Rococo Revival instigated by Empress Eugénie.

MODERNE

A fascination with the new has always been a factor in the French decorative arts: it keeps things moving forward, keeps them fresh. When we use the French word '*moderne*' here it is in this sense of the new and the novel, rather than as a reference to the international Modern Movement.

Modernism in terms of the early twentieth-century international movement is not really an ingredient of the typical Paris interior. As regards furniture, certainly, the French view tends to be that modernism failed to deliver its promise of better and affordable

Faced with an overwhelming number of historical references – from Louis Quatorze, Louis Quinze and Louis Seize to Napoleon, Directoire and the Belle Epoque – it is tempting to assume that the Paris interior must be entirely retrospective in its approach to style. It is true that the French are preoccupied with their history, but it is also true that the main factor that has kept the French decorative arts vibrant and dynamic is their ability to be always changing. They do not do so, however, at the expense of the past.

design for the masses. Le Corbusier (1887–1965) and Charlotte Perriand (1903–99), of course, produced some remarkable designs, but they have ended up being nearly as expensive as antiques. This fact – manufactured tubular steel at prices on a par with atelier pieces – possibly explains why Parisians have tended not to put modernist design on a pedestal, despite the best attempts of many contemporary architects. Having been at the epicentre of the decorative arts for almost four centuries, Parisians are not an 'easy sell'.

In the courts of the Bourbon kings, invention was as highly prized as virtuosity. André-Charles Boulle (for Louis XIV), Jean-François Oeben (for Louis XV), Jean-Henri Riesener (for Marie Antoinette and Louis XVI) and Georges Jacob (for Marie Antoinette before the Revolution and Napoleon later) made their names by creating new veneers, new forms, new shapes and, in some cases, entirely new kinds of furniture that had not existed previously. None of them got to their position of Ebéniste du Roi, or their position in design history for that matter, by

doing the same as everyone else. They were continually experimenting, pushing their materials to the limit, and investigating new technology, not just because it would please their patrons but because in an age of intense competition, the craftsman who was able to come up with something new was the one who got himself noticed. Whether in cabinetmaking, fabric design, clockmaking or architecture, in the grandest scheme or the smallest detail, new developments were enthusiastically patronized. But it was never at the expense of beauty or quality: all work had to stand up to intense scrutiny. Parisians were never an acquiescing audience: new was not enough. It had to be new and beautiful to capture the imagination.

The French concern for new in the context of luxury, comfort and quality is a powerfully attractive formula. It is not surprising, then, that French designers in the twentieth century – and into the twenty-first – have continued to set the decorative pace.

Jean-Michel Frank (1893–1941), for instance, became a darling of the transatlantic set just before World War II with his pared-down monochromatic interiors. The finest materials, from vellum panelling to limed oak and suede upholstery in natural tones, orchestrated a completely new style of interior by relying on subtle changes of texture for effect. His work, however, was not just 'all beige'. It was luxurious – extravagant even – and had familiar historical undertones.

This in-built sense of continuity is also evident in the work of contemporary Parisian designers. Eric Schmidt, for example, is a sculptor who works in bronze. Not only is he continuing an established tradition of German-born artists/artisans working and thriving in Paris (like Riesener, Oberkampf and Haussmann before him) but also the very material he works in is a reminder of the preferences of the *ancien régime*. He uses it in modern shapes and forms, often reinventing very traditional items such as firedogs or stair banisters; he has even produced a contemporary take on the bronze

fountainhead. The interior designer Frédéric Méchiche, meanwhile, is celebrated for his work combining select elements of Parisian history – for example, an entire room of eighteenth-century panelling – with avant-garde works of art. Like Marie Antoinette, he challenges the accepted convention without being so unusual as to become absurd. There is, notably, an aristocratic discipline to this sort of innovation that designers in Paris, more than elsewhere, seem to have perfected.

created in 1954 in order to perpetuate the tradition of French excellence in the decorative arts – produce numerous classic designs which have been favourites with many generations. But most of these firms also have design studios that maintain a constant quest for 'the next classic'; to this end they are not afraid to go down some very experimental roads. Even if the quest is not always rewarded with commercial success, they remain committed to both quality and innovation.

Whether it is Christian Tortu's highly original but strangely familiar vases or Christian Liaigre's pared-down but nonetheless luxurious and exotic furniture, innovation and invention are much in evidence in contemporary Parisian design. But at the same time it adheres to the rules established during the reigns of Louis XIV, XV and XVI – namely the importance of quality, beauty and practicality. This is evident, too, in the contemporary products of France's long-established luxury manfacturers. Companies such as Christofle, Daum, Hermès, Lalique, Louis Vuitton, Puiforcat and Sèvres – all established for more than two centuries and now members of the Comité Colbert, an organization

The role of the *moderne* in the Paris interior is not to be underestimated. The past is indeed compelling – as many of the pictures in this book show – but the new is undoubtedly the source of vitality. As François Mathey so aptly summarizes in her preface to the book *L'Art de Vivre*: 'Paris grasped the point that a classically conformist unity of style engenders boredom, and that good taste can easily become oppressive. The past delights both mind and eye and should not be overlooked, but if the quality of life is to be maintained, both mind and eye are in need of constant refreshment'. The way this 'refreshment' is presented is what sets Paris *moderne* apart.

Prior to the twentieth century the fireplace was the focal point of the French interior; as well as being the primary source of heat it was also important as a source of light. Considering its significance, it is not surprising that the fireplace received a great deal of aesthetic attention; this applied not just to the marble or stone surrounding it but also to the firedogs inside. The French aristocracy expended considerable sums in commissioning these mini-sculptures – often fashioned from gilded bronze – to support the burning logs. With these contemporary bronze firedogs, Parisian sculptor Eric Schmidt has continued the tradition, albeit in a completely modern idiom.

Only the most stately homes in Paris would have had gardens. The design of these rare spaces was therefore perhaps even more considered than the decoration of an interior. For the smaller *parterre* garden, the preferred approach was one of formality, symmetry and order. It was a design concept that had been perfected by Louis XIV and Le Nôtre at Versailles; from grand examples such as this Parisians learned the importance of sculpture and the use of areas of green to delineate space. It is an approach that seems to work equally well whether the sculpture is classical in origin or abstract and modern – as in the case of this bronze fountainhead by Eric Schmidt.

Black-and-white photographs by Lartigue, hanging on early nineteenth-century boiserie: the juxtaposition is typical of the Parisian approach to modern design, which works with the immense historical precedent of Parisian culture rather than ignoring it.

Distinct design tendencies have recurred throughout the history of the French decorative arts – reappearing perhaps in a different expression, but consistent all the same. A penchant for asymmetrical, organic shapes can be seen in the Rococo or Louis Quinze style, and in the Art Nouveau of the late nineteenth century. The modernism of the 1950s produced another variation on the same theme, as illustrated by this silver bowl and vase.

As horse-drawn carriages became obsolete there was an unexpected advantage for owners of nineteenth-century Parisian mansions or *hôtels particuliers*. Neither the *porte cochère* (the long covered passage on the side of the house through which the carriage would enter) nor the courtyard behind it (essential for turning the carriage around) were needed any longer. This created the perfect location for a courtyard garden. Mostly similar in size and shape, these spaces were particularly suited to the introduction of novel design approaches.

Moderne, in the context of the Paris interior, means a concern for the new and the innovative rather than a reference to twentieth-century modernism. Since the time of Louis XIV the French have been faithful patrons of innovation; it is a trend that continues today on a small scale as well as on a monumental one. The approach of designer Frédéric Méchiche is to mix key elements of French decorative history with pieces of avant-garde modern art. In this case, late eighteenth-century mauve-coloured walls and a Jeff Koons dog – a miniature variation on his floral 'sculpture' in front of the Guggenheim Museum in Bilbao – combine in a classical hallway niche in a Paris apartment.

In the seventeenth century clocks were a new scientific phenomenon, embraced with equal enthusiasm by the English, Dutch, Germans, Austrians and Italians. But it was the French who took clockmaking to unprecedented heights. As in other disciplines associated with design and decoration, it was the French – centred on Paris – who dominated the clockmaker's craft.

Louis XIV (1638–1715) gave his most accomplished clockmakers permanent lodgings in the Palais du Louvre. Their status as *artistes* afforded them rare privileges: they were allowed access to the king, and dined in the palace at the table of the Gentlemen of the Chamber. As well as carrying out feats of craftsmanship and decoration, the clockmaker was an indispensable part of the king's routine: every morning he would wind up the king's clocks and adjust the fob watch he was about to wear.

Resident at the palace in Louis XIV's time was his Ebéniste du Roi, the cabinetmaker André-Charles Boulle (1642–1732). His dramatic use of brass, tortoiseshell, mother-of-pearl and ormolu – a bronzed metal alloy created to simulate gold – was perfectly in step with the Sun King's ornate Baroque taste. If it was grand, elaborate and extravagant, Louis XIV loved it. Boulle turned his attention to clocks as well as cabinets, becoming quite famous for his lively and inventive creations. There is even a typical Boulle clock depicted in Antoine Watteau's well-known painting *L'Enseigne de Gersaint* (1721, State Museum of Berlin).

One of the best clock anecdotes surrounding Louis XIV must surely be the story about the timepiece created for him by Burdeau, another of his clockmakers. This elaborate gilt-brass clock featured a mechanism whereby various European princes and electors would emerge just before the hour chime and bow down to the French monarch. This being a highly political clock, one of the figures was designed to bow lower to the King of France than did the others: this was King William III of England, well known for his opposition to Louis XIV, and whom the Roi du Soleil was known to detest. The clock was naturally a great success at court, but disaster struck when the king arranged for it to be shown to the public.

t was due to strike the hour, the clock's King of France ended up lying prostrate at the feet of William III. The king, needless to say, was not amused, and poor Burdeau's lodgings were quickly moved from the Louvre to the Bastille.

As could be expected – and in line with other French decorative arts – French taste in clocks followed that of whichever Louis happened to be on the throne at the time. The eighteenth century, a time when the unrestrained indulgence of the French court dominated all matters of style, was an especially fertile time for exotic clockmaking.

French clocks, especially mantel clocks, were often remarkable, but it was the fashion for the Rococo during the reign of Louis XV (1710–74; reigned from 1723) that took clockmaking to new extremes. Shells, scrolls and luxurious vegetation were arranged in a fanciful confusion of arabesques that sought to avoid symmetry at all costs. Rococo provided playful relief from Louis XIV's heavy and overbearing Baroque style, reflecting the changing political climate. An accounting book entry by one of Louis XV's Horlogers du Roi, a certain Monsieur Pinon, describing some work done for the Comte d'Artois (the king's brother), sums up nicely the French aristocracy's indulgent attitude during the reign of Louis XV: 'For repairing a movement of a clock in the Prince's apartment, and renewing, in fine bronze, the female figure of the clock-case, which the Prince had amused himself in scratching with a knife from one end to the other, with the object of cleaning it ...'.

Yet despite the decadence and frivolity, this was a tremendously productive period for French artisans in general, and clockmakers in particular. Perhaps it was because the nobility had nothing better to do than amuse themselves with commissioning ever more fanciful pieces in the hope of entertaining themselves and their friends – an eighteenth-century version of designer-label shopping. Whatever the reason, the creative climate produced some remarkable talent.

Possibly the most dazzling personality amongst Louis XV's clockmakers was Pierre-Augustin Caron de Beaumarchais (1732–99), who was not only an award-winning member of the Paris Academy of Sciences but also taught the harp to Louis XV's daughters and wrote two highly successful plays, *The Barber of Seville* and *The Marriage of Figaro*. Scientist, musician, author – these were the credentials of an age when

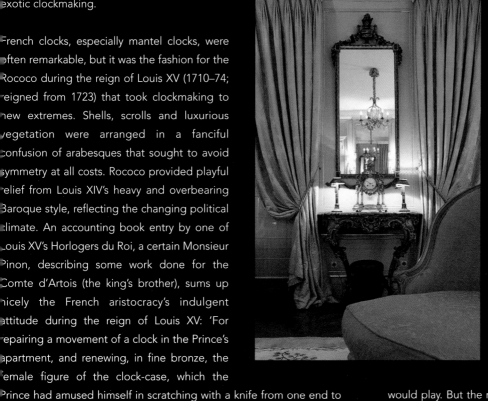

greatest single clockmaking achievement of the Rococo era, however, was undoubtedly the elaborate astronomical clock designed by Admiral Passemont for Louis XV. It took 20 years for Passemont to calculate the clock's various movements and, under his direction, another 12 to build it. This extraordinary clock is still a fixture at the Palace of Versailles, where it was installed in 1750.

Fashion at court was bound to change and towards the end of Louis XV's reign, Rococo had become scrolled and vegetative, to a point where it had become little more than a parody of itself. The return to classicism that characterized the reign of Louis XVI influenced clockmaking as it did furniture, carpets, tapestries, fabrics and even doorknobs. Classical shapes and motifs were everywhere, from urn-like clocks in Sèvres porcelain adorned with gilt-bronze Neoclassical figurines, to lyre-shaped timepieces where the lyre strings formed part of the pendulum. The new taste was simpler, it is true, but it was no less indulgent. The only thing that had changed was the shape – the extravagance remained undiluted.

The eighteenth century in France saw much stylish clockmaking, and the reign of Louis XVI (1754–93; reigned 1774–91) and his queen Marie Antoinette (1755–93) was no exception. Appealing to Marie Antoinette's love of whimsy, a birdcage clock was made where at every hour birds would sing and a fountain would play. But the most dramatic example of eccentric clockmaking at the French court would have to be the bronze head of a Negro woman – also made for Marie Antoinette – where the hour hand is displayed in one eye and the minute hand in the other. It must have been a great success at court because four others were made exactly like it; one of them still keeps time at Buckingham Palace.

Demand for clocks decreased somewhat in the years following the French Revolution – the guillotine had done away with much of the original client base – but such was the strength of clockmaking talent that artisan skills managed to outlast the chaos. Indeed, even when Paris was in complete turmoil – amidst unruly crowds, public executions, seizures and arrests – another decorative theme was emerging. For a short time, the Revolution itself acted as inspiration for Parisian craftsmen, and patriotic emblems – including the cap of liberty, the *trois couleurs* and even the guillotine – featured in paintings, on fabrics, on porcelain and, of course, on clocks.

In any case, it was not long before Napoleon Bonaparte (1769–1821) picked up where the Bourbon kings had left off. As self-appointed Emperor of France, he simply substituted a new colour scheme and changed the motif. Many of the *ébénistes* and *horlogers* who had worked for the court of Louis XVI were now engaged by Napoleon, producing equally sumptuous pieces but now in what became known as the Empire style. Large golden eagles, Cuban mahogany and plenty of swans and bees (gold ones of course) were enlisted on all manner of furniture, including clocks, to celebrate the glory of the new emperor. Despite a bloody revolution, it seemed that little had changed.

Subtlety was not Napoleon's strong point. Art, like everything else, was to be in the service of his empire, as he made clear in a letter to General Daru in 1805: 'My aim is to make the Arts address subjects that will keep alive the memory of

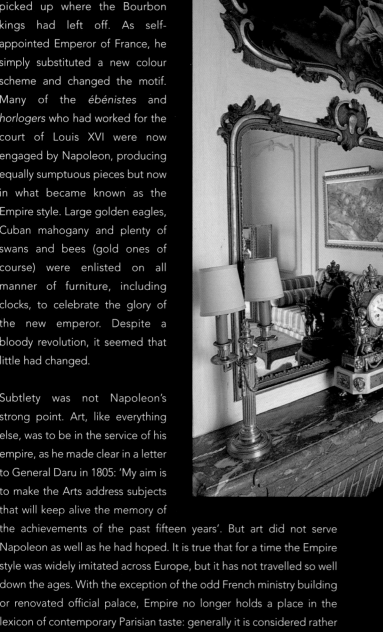

As the nineteenth century unfolded it became increasingly cluttered with a confusing eclecticism. Revivals came thick and fast: Napoleon III was partial to Louis Seize, Rococo briefly returned to fashion, chinoiserie became a dominant theme once more (as it had been throughout the eighteenth century) and the powerful and colourfully eclectic style known as the Belle Epoque mixed it all together. It was a good time for clockmaking, however. Not that the level of invention and craftsmanship ever regained the standards set by the *ancien régime*, but the emergence of a middle class in France and elsewhere in Europe sent demand soaring. Clocks became a big export business for France, and their important role in the Paris interior was established once and for all. The quantity of clocks produced at this time accounts for the large number of antique pieces that are still available from *antiquaires*, flea markets and auction houses. As with Louis

the achievements of the past fifteen years'. But art did not serve Napoleon as well as he had hoped. It is true that for a time the Empire style was widely imitated across Europe, but it has not travelled so well down the ages. With the exception of the odd French ministry building or renovated official palace, Empire no longer holds a place in the lexicon of contemporary Parisian taste: generally it is considered rather *nouveau riche*. Nevertheless, from an artisan's point of view it was at least a cohesive style, with a unity in ornament and decoration – which is more than can be said for the rest of the century.

Quinze and Louis Seize chairs, nineteenth-century clockmakers were quite content to copy pieces from the preceding century, and thus a hierarchy of authenticity exists, with pieces made in the eighteenth century at the very top of the scale.

Unlike other aspects of the Paris interior, the clock did not reinvent or reinterpret itself in the twentieth century. The clocks that typify the Parisian interior today are antiques – beautiful survivors of a time when science and art collaborated so successfully.

Christiaan Huygens' invention of the pendulum in The Hague in 1657 not only introduced a new accuracy in time-keeping but also necessitated the creation of a new form to house this revolutionary mechanism. As with most decorative disciplines, Louis XIV was a pioneer. But the Sun King's interest was not only aesthetic. Recognizing the keeping of time as a science, he established the Académie Royale des Sciences in Paris in 1664. Huygens became a member, and in 1673 dedicated his *Horologium Oscillatorium* to the king. The clock shown here, with its fine gilded metal dial, enamel cartouches and gilded bronze fittings, is a typical example from the late 1600s and early 1700s.

In the eighteenth century, clocks did not so much tell the time as surround it. The importance of the mantel clock was reinforced by the extraordinary decorative effort lavished on it. The French clock was fine art, craftsmanship and science rolled into one.

The clocks of the *ancien regime* are 'like small pieces of historical architecture, providing a glimpse of the design evolution that occurred from period to period and throne to throne. Louis Quatorze-style cartel clocks – typified by the example that opens this chapter – were modified under Louis XV, but the basic shape did not alter too much. The real change was in the detail. Cases would now often be finished in *vernis Martin* (green in this example); the gilded bronze decoration would be more asymmetrical than previously and would feature flowers instead of classical figures.

The small clock independent of a grand decorative scheme (that is, not conceived by an architect to fit into a master plan) became popular from the mid-eighteenth century. These clocks were tableaux in themselves, small pieces of plastic art with motifs and mounts that reinforced their status as an independent aesthetic statement. The monumentality of the decorative figures was often reinforced by a heroic choice of theme: in this case a putti (cherub) surmounts a pair of lions. Through all the changes in style, however, the fundamentals stayed the same: dial and hand divide up the time.

Around the end of the seventeenth century a new style of fireplace emerged in France, comprising a vertical smoke stack over which was hung a looking-glass panel. The area in front of the mirror became the accepted location for a pendulum clock.

At first all pendulum clocks looked almost exactly the same, whether they came from the Netherlands, England or France. Within a short space of time, however, the decorative preferences of these different cultures began to assert themselves. By the 1750s, French clocks intended for the mantle had developed into a form of visual expression that was entirely independent of the mechanics of the clock. This pendulum clock, set in a case of finely detailed gilded bronze, is typical of the more restrained expression of Rococo popular in the late 1750s.

The invention of the pendulum introduced new requirements to the placement of a clock. To maintain accuracy the pendulum had to swing in a vertical plane, which required a stable position. And so the clock went from being an object without any fixed location to one that sat on a mantel or was attached firmly to the wall.

Two cartel clocks, one of them Louis Quatorze and the other Louis Quinze, illustrate the changes imposed by the different decorative periods. The Louis Quatorze example, on the left, is all symmetry, mounted on what was known as *boulle* (walnut veneer). The Louis Quinze piece, by contrast, is more 'organic' in its decorative inspiration, featuring elaborately sculptural bronze mounts with asymmetrical flourishes.

By the 1730s the elaborate boiseries and illusionary ceilings associated with the taste of Louis XIV had all but disappeared. Figurative decoration was from here on more or less confined to portraits, to panels above doors and fireplaces, and – of course – to clocks. With their splendid decorative scenes these timepieces were variously intended to reflect the atmosphere of a room or the glory of the king – and more often than not the good taste of the owner. Individuality was entering the domestic equation, via the clock. In this case, the taste was for chinoiserie.

In the nineteenth century, standardization allowed clocks to be made in ever greater quantities. Soon it was almost unheard of not to have a clock in every room. It was a development that attracted the kind of criticism reserved for television and the Internet today. In the words of one contemporary writer: 'Since there is neither utility or pleasure in these meaningless forms and costly manufactures, one can only groan at the waste of money'. Sounds familiar?

The decoration of French clocks reflects the more general taste of the times. During the last decade of Louis XV's rule, as people started to reject the increasingly fanciful nature of Rococo, classical symbolism started to replace the organic repertoire. Mantel clocks, in particular, became more symmetrical and began to feature classical motifs such as swags and urns.

A tight close-up of a cartel clock from the late seventeenth century reveals the extraordinary level to which French craftsmen took the job of clockmaking. No wonder so many specialized artisans were involved in the manufacture of one piece. The quality was the result of a very thorough division of work involving 15 different workshops. There was the *fondeur* to cast the wheel and the plates, the *faiseur de mouvement* to machine all moving parts, the *finisseur* to polish them prior to assembly, and then the enamellers, engravers, cabinetmakers, gilders, the *metteur en couleur* – responsible for

TOILES

Gros de Tours, toile de Jouy, pékiné, siamoise, taffeta à la Chine, lamé ... a run through the names of some of France's best-known and most highly prized decorative fabrics hints at the importance of French textiles within the history of the decorative arts.

France benefited from an early start. Archive records show that tapestries with simple motifs were being woven in Paris and Arras from 1300. With enthusiastic patronage from French and Burgundian royalty tapestry-making expanded rapidly, and by the end of the century both cities were exporting these new 'luxury products' all over Europe. Arras, in particular, was so renowned that its name became synonymous with the product: in Italy tapestry is today still called *arazzo*.

In a world just beginning to emerge from the turmoil of the Middle Ages, tapestries offered some relief from the harsh realities of everyday life. Not only did they help stop draughts, being thick, large and heavy, but they also often represented the only form of pictorial image in a domestic interior. The tapestry was thus both art and insulation – and sometimes a political tool, too. For example, Philip the Good, Duke of Burgundy (1396–1467), notorious for his love of display and his penchant for self-promotion, owned a huge tapestry called *The History of Gideon* which he would hang over the facade of the Hôtel d'Arbois when he was staying in Paris. It is said that Parisians would queue day and night to be able to see it.

A tapestry was a big investment – it demanded a highly skilled, highly organized and highly paid workforce, and thus rich patrons. As the focus of the Burgundian court shifted to Brussels in the second half of the fifteenth century, the city became an important centre of artistic patronage. The Flemish weavers of Brussels were to dominate the extremely lucrative tapestry market for more than a hundred years, until the French king Henri IV (1533–1610) made a bid to re-establish dominance in Paris. Shrewdly taking advantage of the wars and

religious persecution (at the hands of the Spanish) that were taking place in the Netherlands, Henri IV established an industry in Paris staffed almost exclusively with Flemish weavers whom he had lured away from the turbulence and uncertainty of Brussels. Not only was Henri's venture a resounding success, reclaiming Paris as the premier source of fine tapestries, but it also set an important precedent for French royal patronage.

task was to find or create suitable designs. These 'cartoons' were to feature either Louis XIV in person – as in the series *L'histoire du Roi* – or heroic figures from mythology or history which the king could identify with. It was perhaps the ultimate example of the Sun King's egocentric approach: Les Gobelins was financed by the king to create superior tapestries, only for himself, featuring himself, with which he could then decorate his own residences.

Henri IV's son, Louis XIII (1601–43), dutifully continued with his father's enterprise but it was the next Louis, Louis XIV (1638–1715), who was to take it to a new level, redefining the whole idea of the *manufacture royale*. In 1662 Jean-Baptiste Colbert, Louis XIV's chief minister, brought together under one roof all the weaving ateliers started by Henri IV. He moved them to a site in Paris called Les Gobelins and handed creative direction to his First Painter, Charles Le Brun (1619–90). It was the beginning of the Sun King's singular approach to patronage. The production of Les Gobelins was reserved exclusively for the king (for the decoration of his numerous palaces), and Le Brun's

Louis XIV's self-aggrandizing antics may have bordered on the farcical, yet it seems that the more outrageous he became the more he was imitated. Following his example, tapestries became increasingly fashionable throughout Europe and with Les Gobelins working exclusively for the king, commercial demand was accommodated by the looms of Beauvais and Aubusson. The Sun King's extravagance had created an export industry. What is more astonishing is that his idea of a personal, private tapestry workshop caught on too. Imagine all the barons, princes, counts, queens and kings of other European courts at the time, gossiping to each other: 'Have you heard? Louis has his own

tapestry atelier. How terribly chic – I want one too!' And soon enough there were set-ups similar to Les Gobelins springing up in Rome, Munich, Madrid, Naples and St Petersburg.

Louis XIV's role in the development of French textiles was not confined to grand patronage, however. With his 'divine right', he saw his role as not just to nurture and promote industries in which the French excelled but also to prohibit any that he viewed as a potential threat. He was certainly not above a bit of heavy-handed bullying to get his way, as is graphically demonstrated by the story of silk in France. By the mid-seventeenth century, the French silk-weaving industry was producing the finest and most spectacular silks in the world. Lyons, in particular, was considered superior to all other European centres because of the quality and diversity of its repertoire, which ranged from plain satin to taffeta to very elaborate brocade with metallic thread. There was a cause of great concern for French silk manufacturers, however: the growing popularity of brightly coloured printed cottons

brought back from the Indian subcontinent by the East India Company and copied by some French workshops. As their alarm at the competition grew, silk producers put pressure on the government to intervene.

Louis XIV was happy to oblige: in 1686 he banned not only the import of cotton cloth from India but also the production of printed imitations. Henceforth, printed cotton was illegal in France – and it stayed that way for almost three-quarters of a century. The French silk industry had the protection it wanted, but it remains questionable whether such action was really necessary. From the 1650s up until the mid-nineteenth century, French silk stood head and shoulders above its rivals both in terms of design novelty and what can only be described as a sense of 'good taste'. Despite the fact that the Italians had been weaving silk since the first eggs of the mulberry silk moth were smuggled in from China in the sixth century, it was the French who dominated the market. The choice of French silks was simply bewildering. Early in the eighteenth century, for example, there was a fashion for 'bizarre' silks featuring Oriental motifs in startling colour combinations such as pink

with green and brown, or violet with grey and green. From the 1730s onwards each decade seemed to be marked by a major change in design direction – a relentless cycle of taste that no doubt lay behind the quip by the English parliamentarian and wit Horace Walpole that 'fashion [in France] lasts no longer than a lover'.

The 1730s also marked the emergence of the first 'superstar' among the Lyonnais silk designers: Jean Revel (1684–1751). Revel introduced a new style, one with which his name is still associated today, comprising oversized, three-dimensional compositions of fruit and flowers that dwarf the figures and architectural features also present in the design. To truly understand how revolutionary these silk designers and manufacturers could be, however, we should look to the work of Philippe de Lasalle (1723–1805), a giant of the Lyons silk industry who counted amongst his clients and admirers the Tsar of Russia and Marie Antoinette. His designs belie the fact that they were created in the eighteenth century; he has even been credited with the invention of the fake fur motif. One of his creations, a salmon-pink silk with pink, white and faux-leopardskin stripes, would no doubt be considered a bold, courageous and very funky choice even today. Yet this fabric emerged at a time when North American settlers were still chopping down trees to build rudimentary log cabins. No wonder the sophisticated French – and Parisians in particular of course – were regarded with such awe!

The dominance of and favouritism given to French silk was not without its drawbacks, however: most notably it resulted in the total atrophy of the cotton textile industry in France. Louis XIV's decree was not lifted until 1759 (well into the reign of Louis XV), by which time other countries such as Britain and Germany had made great strides forward in cotton manufacturing. A new printing technique, for example, had been developed in Dublin using engraved copper plates rather than the earlier time-consuming and unreliable wooden blocks. This invention was soon brought over to England, and for well over two decades London and Dublin enjoyed a monopoly on these cottons. The one drawback of copper-plate printing was that the fine engraving it required could only take one colour, hence it could only be printed in monochrome. However, this became a distinguishing feature of the cloth and one of its great attractions.

After 70-odd years of prohibition, France lacked experience and skills in printed cotton. Amid rapidly growing demand, the only solution was to do what Henri IV had done with tapestry in the sixteenth century: lure the talent from elsewhere. In this case it was the expertise of printers from Germany, Holland and Switzerland that was called upon. It was thus that Christophe-Philippe Oberkampf (1738–1815), a German citizen living and working in Switzerland, was invited to Paris in 1758 to help establish some print works. Two years later Oberkampf

did not take long for *toiles de Jouy* (fabric from Jouy) to win widespread recognition. By 1783, with Jean-Baptiste Huet (1745–1811) as chief designer, Oberkampf's high-quality engravings were being widely imitated in France as well as abroad and the Jouy works was granted the title of *manufacture royale*. At a time when a preference for anything other than silk was considered nothing short of a betrayal of aristocratic taste, Marie Antoinette scandalously revealed her penchant for *toiles de Jouy* by specifying these trademark printed cottons for her *hameau* (hamlet) at Versailles. It was a stamp of approval that not only sparked off a whole new fashion – as the queen's taste was apt to do – but also helped establish *toile de Jouy* as an enduring element of the typical French interior.

Even during the French Revolution, Oberkampf's business thrived – now involved in printing scenes that were rich in revolutionary symbolism. In the early years of the subsequent Empire period, Napoleon added to Oberkampf's accolades by awarding him the Légion d'honneur. This was in spite of the emperor's well-known patronage of the Lyons silk industry: in an effort to revive an industry that had been decimated by the abolition of its number one client – the French nobility – Napoleon, in a manner not so far removed from Louis XIV, ordered huge quantities of silk to decorate the various palaces left empty in the years following the Revolution. When Napoleon fell from power in 1815, the *mobilier impérial* had in stock 68 kilometres of unused silk – a quantity so vast that French rulers were able to use it for decoration of official buildings until 1960.

Today the term *toile de Jouy* generally refers to a particular style of fabric – a monochrome cotton with figurative design – wherever it may be made. (While silkscreen imitations abound in France and abroad, one French manufacturer still produces fabric using some of the original Oberkampf plates – a remarkable survival.) To this day the fabric remains a ubiquitous ingredient of the Parisian interior: a design element that is quintessentially French. Silk, too, and even tapestry, to a more limited degree, have also survived the rigours of historical selection, and feature in some of today's most stylish Parisian decors. The legacy of French virtuosity with fabric can be viewed in the same way that we might regard classical music: an achievement brought about by unique circumstances of history, which we can reproduce today but do not have the skills to improve upon.

Of all the French fabrics, silk in its various guises – damask, brocade, *bazin, pékiné and siamoise* to name but a few – enjoyed the greatest prestige and the greatest degree of patronage from France's absolute rulers. For interiors of the *ancien régime,* the type of silk was determined by both function and season. Heavier silks such as this satin damask – distinguished by a three-dimensional relief cut into the fabric with acid – would have been used for curtains.

Although the French were late in developing their own printed cotton industry, once they did so it did not take them long to reach a position where they dominated the market. Part of the credit must go to the phenomenally successful *toiles de Jouy,* the monochrome printed cotton from Christophe-Philippe Oberkampf's factory in Jouy, outside Paris. With a great variety of designs executed by well-known French artists of the day, such as Jean-Baptiste Huet and Jean-Baptiste Pillement, Oberkampf created a particular style of fabric that went on to become quintessentially French – even though the technique of manufacture was invented in Ireland.

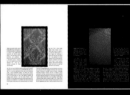

Stylized motifs of intertwined garlands or vines are typical of the patterns that were popular in the time of Louis XVI. The main *soyeur* at the time was a company called Tassinari & Chatel, who today still supply the official palaces of France.

Water-stained silk, or moiré, is another fabric that the French have made so much their own that people forget that it was invented elsewhere – this time in England.

It was Napoleon Bonaparte who instigated the fashion for rooms hung with silks. To resurrect the ailing Lyons silk industry, he ordered extraordinary quantities to redecorate all his palaces – and also set off a new fashion among the European aristocracy (despite the Revolution, France was still seen as the leader in matters of taste and style). But Bonaparte may have been a bit overzealous with his quantities: when he fell from power the *mobilier impérial* had 68 kilometres of silk left in stock. The bedroom shown here is hung with a plain coloured water-stained silk, while the silk bedspread features fashionable Neo-classical motifs.

Although the Italians originally dominated the silk industry in Europe, the patronage of Louis XIV – organized with great skill by his chief minister Colbert – saw to it that France eventually had the upper hand. At Louis' instigation strong emphasis was placed on technological advancement: it was not just a matter of what was made, but how it was made.

48.ᵉ

Mon lit d'acelle Lefebure en afaïance

N8^d

a bronze fitting. To us it may seem overbearingly bureaucratic, but in its day the system served the cause of craftsmanship very well. It was as if King Louis XIV and his minister Colbert – who was responsible for making the guilds a matter of legislation – knew that an artisan who was restricted by law to making only marquetry panels, would try to make them the most extraordinary examples of marquetry ever seen. Most artisans, they rightly assumed, would work to the very limits of their own strictly regulated category. Intense specialization, established and supervised by the state, inevitably led to extremely high-quality workmanship and elaborate detail.

But to attribute the extraordinary attention to decorative detail that was found in pre-Revolutionary France solely to a state-supervised system of craft specialization, would be to ignore another important factor: the idle capriciousness of the French elite. Members of the

istocracy generally had little to do other than think of new ways of making use of the vast pool of creative talent that was at their disposal – and surely no one more so than Louis XVI's queen, Marie Antoinette 1755–93). She had the handles of some of her gilded armchairs carved n the shape of her favourite lap dog, while her bathroom, commissioned from Richard Mique, was decorated in an exquisitely carved scheme incorporating fountains, dolphins, lobsters, swans, shells and white coral. Added to this were the *hameau*, *laiterie* and Petit Trianon that she had built at Versailles, and her Neo-classical gold-and-white apartments at Fontainebleau. These lavish decorative and architectural schemes were, for Marie Antoinette, simply *amusant*.

This peculiarly French combination – of strictly managed and well-organized craft disciplines fuelled by the pursuit of eccentric, extravagant personal indulgence – proved to be a recurrent theme. It not only survived the French Revolution but would ultimately serve as the very foundation of the country's luxury industry. Even though the guilds were dissolved during the Revolution, many ateliers survived. Their skills were handed down to the next generation, who found fresh clientele in the newly moneyed bourgeoisie. Napoleon Bonaparte (1769–1821) and his wife Joséphine, who once in power basically behaved no differently from the monarchy, made use of these skills in order to decorate palaces that had been looted during the Revolution. Napoleon also attempted to revive an economy that was in shambles by supporting and promoting national industries that had been founded under the *ancien régime*, such as Sèvres porcelain and Aubusson tapestries, and by helping to establish new ones in crystalware, jewellery, leatherware and silverware, for example.

By the time of Napoleon's final exile in 1815, France had established an industrial base that was unlike any other: it was founded on the premise of painstakingly handcrafted items of unparalleled design

made in quantity. Employing highly skilled craftsmen, these factories specialized in making established designs by hand, and in large numbers to cater for growing demand at home and abroad. Customers preferred these products, hand-made in quantity, to the one-off item because they had an established design provenance. Hand-making the same item over and over again subjected the design and detail to intense scrutiny. It had to be exactly right ... and it was. The stemware that crystal manufacturer Baccarat first introduced in 1841 is still one of the company's most popular designs. In fact, a recent report on retail consumption in France noted that an astonishing 75 per cent of luxury purchases for the home still come from traditional French brands such as Baccarat, Saint-Louis, Christofle and Daum.

In these industries, the slightest nuance, the smallest detail can make all the difference between success and failure. With these companies having been part of French society for one-and-a-half centuries, certain expectations have been handed down through the generations. Although today many of them are quite large concerns making a significant contribution to France's economy as well as to the prestige the country is accorded around the globe, they still operate in a manner not that dissimilar to Les Gobelins, the tapestry atelier established by Louis XIV in the seventeenth century. No attempt has been made to replace the time-consuming, craft-intensive, hand-made component with a machine – and the most popular designs have changed very little down the years. Thus, not only is attention to detail a hand-me-down from the imposing history of the decorative arts in France but it is also firmly entrenched as a *modus operandi* in the luxury products industry. Whether it is in the saddle-stitching on a contemporary leather sofa or the intricate cut of a cactus-shaped stopper on a crystal decanter, the perfection of hand-crafted detail is as much part of the Paris interior as it was in the time of the pre-Revolutionary guilds.

Ribbons, fruit, leaves, branches and garlands ... these are typical ornaments of the Rococo (Louis Quinze) style. Whereas in the eighteenth century such motifs would have been carved in wood, the late nineteenth century saw them transferred to plaster. Moulded or carved plaster panels such as this were used to adorn the area directly above a doorway.

In homage to the craft of the eighteenth-century *ciseleur*, even the handles of window bars benefit from the minutest attention to detail. In this case the design inspiration is the fondness for grotesques that typified the Baroque style of Louis XIV. A catalogue published by Maison R. Garnier in the late 1800s features pages and pages of window and door handles in every style imaginable. A plain handle would have been a wasted opportunity.

Although the Royal German workshop of Meissen, near Dresden, first 'cracked the code' of how Chinese porcelain was made, it was the factory patronized by the Bourbon kings that took its design and decoration to another level. Even after the Revolution, Sèvres porcelain was so revered that Napoleon used it as a tool of foreign diplomacy: if a country was important to France's political ambitions, their head of state received a complete set of exquisite hand-painted dinnerware. (The United States had to wait almost four decades until it was deemed important enough for its president to eat off Sèvres.) Almost all the original designs – which were done full scale – are preserved at the archives of the Musée de Sèvres.

Fluted pilasters, Corinthian capitals, acanthus leaves ... the architectural language of the ancients also provided the ingredients for Louis Seize-style Neo-classicism. The city planner Baron Haussmann revived these features in the nineteenth century, during the Second Empire of Napoleon III. His prescribed formula, which governed both the height of the buildings and the type of architectural detailing, has given Paris a uniformity and visual cohesion that no other international capital can match.

Fer forgé (wrought iron) made an important contribution to the French lexicon of decorative expression. Gates, railings and handrails were treated with as much regard for design and detail as were the most exquisite pieces of furniture or the finest silks. One does not necessarily have to look at a complex piece to see the level of artistry that went into this craft: this close-up of a railing highlights the decorative success of one simple gilded detail.

Despite the distinction drawn between the Louis Quatorze and Louis Quinze styles, there existed a substantial degree of overlap. Many ingredients of one style became the hand-me-down of the next. For instance, the use of gilded bronze mounts depicting mythological figures (often given recognizable features), a fashion that Louis XIV was particularly fond of, continued throughout the reign of the Bourbon kings.

A *lumière* – literally, a 'source of light' – was the popular name given to a crystal chandelier in the eighteenth and nineteenth centuries, and its easy to see why. Utilizing an artistic arrangement of glass beads and drops, the entire composition would reflect and amplify the light emanating from the candles it was designed to hold.

The mirror, or looking-glass as it was known in the eighteenth century, had been the jealously guarded preserve of the Venetians – recognized masters of glasswork – until the French invented the technology to produce mirror plates of a size previously unheard of. As with most areas of the decorative arts, the French became totally dominant. The famous Hall of Mirrors at Versailles was, in fact, a very grand and effective advertisement for the French mastery of looking-glass manufacture.

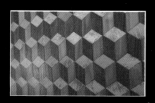

A Rococo balcony railing is composed almost entirely of simple but elegant 'C' scrolls; together with the 'S' scroll this was a fundamental component of the Louis Quinze or Rococo style. The result is testament to the ability of Parisian craftsmen to create something lastingly beautiful out of a very simple repertoire of shapes.

Marquetry, a form of decorative veneering, was practised by specialized craftsman called *ébenistes* who were trained within the highly organized guild system of the *ancien régime*. They learned how to use subtle variations in the grain and colour of different timbers in the same way that a painter would use a palette, creating 'pictures' of great complexity and sophistication. A popular device was the use of geometric arrangements that alter in appearance when the observer changes their angle of view; to the modern eye, the result is strangely reminiscent of an Escher print.

In the eighteenth century candles were expensive, especially those made from beeswax – which were favoured because they had no smell and minimal smoke. As the primary source of light after dark, they were extremely important. The high status of the candle was reflected in the level of adornment and detail invested in candelabra and wall-mounted candle holders.

A grotesque face, with its tongue sticking out, adorns the base of a small vanity mirror. It shows how, in their attention to detail, the French were not without a sense of humour.

Author's acknowledgements

The style of Paris is powerfully seductive, without a doubt, but it is also quite elusive, particularly when it comes to capturing it on camera film. As with most photography, it helps if the model has everything you are looking for. In this case, the model for *The Paris Interior* was a splendid Haussmann-era *hôtel particulier* that originally belonged to a certain Monsieur Wolf – a collector and man of taste, with a broad interest in the history of the French decorative arts – who assembled a collection of superb French clocks as well as some photogenic examples of Louis Quinze and Louis Seize furniture.

But it took the eye of Grace Léo-Andrieu and her team to bring Monsieur Wolf's superb *hôtel particulier* – a splendid Paris interior – into contemporary relevance. With equal measures of modern sensibility and care for the wealth of architectural and decorative historical detail, she has turned Monsieur Wolf's *hôtel particulier* into the highly refined environment that is her Hôtel Lancaster. Parisians have always been as passionate about the new as they have about quality and beauty, and it is this sense of the *moderne* that makes this piece of collective history so seductive today. Contemporary design, new fabrics and state-of-the-art bathrooms combine effortlessly with the *guéridons*, *fauteuils*, *armoires* and *bergères* of the *ancien régime*.

If Grace Leo-Andrieu's superb *hôtel particulier* is responsible for the photography, the credit for presenting these images in a manner so complementary to Parisian style goes to Anthony Michael of Michael Nash Associates. He really understands the ambience of Paris and, most importantly, has managed to translate this into a graphic language. Without his graphic input, *The Paris Interior* would not have progressed beyond being a collection of nice pictures.

Finally, I was going to comment that it is such a pity that books are not as organized as films in acknowledging everyone's contribution, and it struck me that 'organized' is the key word. Thanks to all the people who helped me to organize myself: Wendy Gilliatt of Michael Nash Associates; Caroline Proud, Claire Wrathall and Muna Reyal of Conran Octopus; Christine Davis, my editor; and, of course, Danielle, who is always ready to tackle the bits and pieces that are, at first, far too complex or difficult to contemplate.

Bibliography

Baudot, François.
Empire Style.
London: Thames and Hudson, 1999.

Boyer, Marie-France and Halard, François.
The Private Realm of Marie Antoinette.
London: Thames and Hudson, 1995.

Cliff, Stafford.
The French Archive of Design and Decoration.
London: Thames and Hudson, 1999.

D'Archimbaud, Nicholas, et al.
Versailles.
Paris: Editions du Chêne, 1999.

De Marly, Diana.
Louis XIV and Versailles.
New York: Holmes and Meier, 1987.

Harris, Jennifer.
5,000 Years of Textiles.
London: British Museum Press, 1993.

Haskell, Francis and Penny, Nicholas.
Taste and the Antique.
New Haven and London: Yale University Press, 1981.

Jacobsen, Dawn.
Chinoiserie.
London: Phaidon Press, 1993.

Jullian, Philippe.
Le Style Louis XVI.
Paris: Baschet et Cie, 1983 (reprint).

L'Art de Vivre:
Decorative Arts and Design in France 1789–1989.
London: Thames and Hudson, 1989.

Linley, David.
Classical Furniture.
London: Pavilion Books, 1993.

Litchfield, Frederick.
The Illustrated History of Furniture.
London: Truslove and Hanson, 1907.

McAlpine, Alistair and Giangrande, Cathy.
Collecting and Display.
London: Conran Octopus, 1998.

Mighell, John.
Miller's Antique Checklist: Clocks.
London: Reed International Books, 1992.

Payne, Christopher (ed.).
Sotheby's Concise Encyclopedia of Furniture.
London: Conran Octopus, 1989.

Thornton, Peter.
Decor: The Domestic Interior 1620–1920.
London: Weidenfeld and Nicolson, 1984.

Picture credits

Louis v Louis

Marlene Dietrich, from the film *Shanghai Express*
Don English/Paramount, courtesy of Kobal Collection

Louis XVI, roi de France et de Navarre
Joseph Siffred Duplessis (1725–1802), 1778
Châteaux de Versailles et de Trianon
©Photo RMN/Gérard Blot

Portrait de Louis XV
School of Jean-Baptiste van Loo (1684–1745)
Château de Bois
©Photo RMN/H. Lewandowski

La famille de Louis XIV en 1670 représentée en travestis mythologiques
Jean Nocret (1617–1672), 1670
Châteaux de Versailles et de Trianon
©Photo RMN

Chinoiserie

Le jardin chinois
François Boucher (1703–1770)
Musée des Beaux-Arts, Besançon
©Photo RMN/Gérard Blot

Projet de vantaux de portes
Nicolas Pineau (1684–1754), Eighteenth century
Musée des Arts Décoratifs, Paris
©UCAD

Projet de fauteuil
Nicholas Pineau (1684–1754), circa 1735
Musée des Arts Décoratifs, Paris
©UCAD

Madame Coco Chanel
Hoyningen-Huene, © Horst, courtesy of the Hamilton Gallery Collection

First published in Great Britain in 2000 by Conran Octopus Limited. A part of Octopus Publishing Group. 2–4 Heron Quays, London E14 4JP www.conran-octopus.co.uk. Photographs and text © Herbert Ypma 2000. Design: Michael Nash Associates. Editor: Christine Davis. Production: Suzanne Bayliss. All rights reserved. No part of this book may be reproduced, stored in a retrieval system or transmitted, in any form or by any means, electronic, electrostatic, magnetic tape, mechanical, photocopying, recording or otherwise, without the prior permission in writing of the Publisher. The right of Herbert Ypma to be identified as the author of this work has been asserted by him in accordance with the Copyright, Designs and Patents Act 1988. British Library Cataloguing-in-Publication Data. A catalogue record for this book is available from the British Library. ISBN 1 84091 166 2. Colour origination by Sang Choy International, Singapore. Printed in China